UNOFFICIAL
GUIDES

21st **Century Skills** INNOVATION LIBRARY

FORTNITE:
Skins

V 550 +

ENGES   EVENTS   LOCKER   ITEM SHOP   CAREER   STORE

NA-EAST

Cherry Lake
Not Ready

+80% XP Boost

TEAM RUMBLE
SQUADS

D1472242

Inspect Emote New

CHERRY LAKE PUBLISHING • **ANN ARBOR, MICHIGAN**

by Josh Gregory

Published in the United States of America by Cherry Lake Publishing
Ann Arbor, Michigan
www.cherrylakepublishing.com

Reading Adviser: Marla Conn MS, Ed., Literacy specialist, Read-Ability, Inc.

Library of Congress Cataloging-in-Publication Data
Names: Gregory, Josh, author.
Title: Fortnite. Skins / by Josh Gregory.
Other titles: Skins
Description: Ann Arbor, Michigan : Cherry Lake Publishing, 2019. | Series:
    Unofficial guides | Series: 21st century skills innovation library |
    Includes bibliographical references and index. | Audience: Grade 4 to 6.
Identifiers: LCCN 2019003337 | ISBN 9781534148154 [lib. bdg.] |
    ISBN 9781534151017 (pbk.) | ISBN 9781534149588 (pdf) |
    ISBN 9781534152441 (ebook)
Subjects: LCSH: Fortnite (Video game)—Juvenile literature.
Classification: LCC GV1469.35.F67 G747 2019 | DDC 794.8—dc23
LC record available at https://lccn.loc.gov/2019003337

Cherry Lake Publishing would like to acknowledge the work of the Partnership for
21st Century Learning. Please visit www.p21.org for more information.

Printed in the United States of America
Corporate Graphics

21st **Century Skills** INNOVATION LIBRARY

Contents

Chapter 1

The Wacky World of *Fortnite*

You never know what you'll see next when you jump into a match of *Fortnite*. A man dressed as a cartoon chicken might jump out from his hiding spot inside a bush to battle a woman wearing a

Hiding inside of a bush is a great way to surprise your enemies in *Fortnite*.

A character carrying a live hamster on her back is exactly the kind of silly thing you will get used to seeing in *Fortnite*.

tomato-shaped mask. A garden gnome might zoom through the air using a glider shaped like ketchup and mustard bottles. A football player might use a giant spatula to chop down a tree. A pink, fuzzy teddy bear might suddenly break out into the latest viral dance craze.

Fortnite is set in a wacky world where just about anything can happen. So why does your character look so plain? When you first start playing *Fortnite*, you won't have any control over your character's appearance. In one match, you might be a man with

The Latest Moves

Fortnite's many wacky dance moves are one of the game's most popular and well-known features. You have probably seen people doing them on TV, YouTube, or Twitch. You and your friends might even have learned some of the moves yourself. But do you know where these dance moves came from?

Believe it or not, many of *Fortnite*'s most famous dance moves were not originally created for the game. Some come from music videos. Others were featured in TV shows or viral videos. Some may have been created before you were even born!

In some cases, the original creators of the dances have not been happy about their moves being used in the game. The *Fortnite* **developers** never asked them before putting their dance moves in the game. The dance creators argue that *Fortnite*'s developers should pay them for using their work.

short hair and dark brown skin. In the next, you might be a woman with long hair and lighter tan skin. You don't get to pick. No matter what, your character will be a normal-looking human. He or she will be wearing simple military-like clothing. You will start each match with a basic pickaxe and glider. No other options will be available to you. You won't even be able to perform any fun dance moves.

So why do all the other players look so crazy while you're stuck playing as regular-looking people?

They've been collecting skins, **emotes**, and other features that let them customize their characters in *Fortnite*. Skins are different appearances for your character, weapons, and other things in the game. Emotes are animations your character can perform in-game. There is a huge variety of these things available in *Fortnite*, and collecting them can be a big part of the fun.

Your friends at school might talk about which skins they've unlocked in *Fortnite* and which ones they are trying to get. When you face off against random players online, they might show off skins and emotes you've never seen before. Some skins and emotes are like trophies. They show that a player is skilled at the game or has been playing for a long time. For many players, chasing after cool new customization options is the main reason to play *Fortnite*.

Unlocking new skins, emotes, and other features can be a difficult and time-consuming process. But if you know exactly what to look for, you can avoid wasting time on the items you don't want. Read on to learn the ins and outs of customizing your *Fortnite* character!

Chapter 2

Skins, Emotes, and Everything Else

*F*ortnite's incredibly huge range of customization options can all be sorted into a handful of categories. Each one affects a different part of your character's appearance or some other aspect of the game.

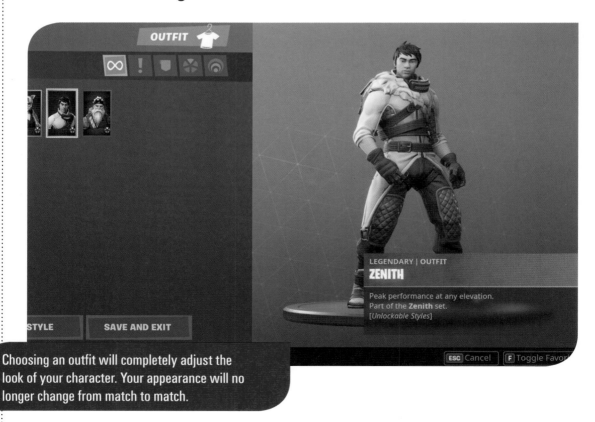

LEGENDARY | OUTFIT
ZENITH

Peak performance at any elevation.
Part of the **Zenith** set.
[*Unlockable Styles*]

Choosing an outfit will completely adjust the look of your character. Your appearance will no longer change from match to match.

One of the biggest ways to change your character's style in *Fortnite* is by equipping different outfits. Outfits are clothing or costumes that your character can wear in the game. Each outfit completely changes your character's appearance from head to toe. So, for example, you can't mix and match different pants and shirts. You can only switch your character's overall look.

Some outfits are fairly simple and don't look all that different from the **default** character appearance. For example, the Commando outfit keeps your character in military-inspired clothing. However, the clothing is a darker color than normal. The Assault Trooper skin gives your character greenish-brown clothing.

Other outfits change your character's look in a much more dramatic way. The Crackshot outfit makes your character look like a holiday nutcracker, complete with a wooden head. The A.I.M. outfit turns your character into a powerful-looking robot. The Giddy-Up outfit makes it look like your character is riding an inflatable llama. In general, the wackier an outfit is, the more *Fortnite* players will want it. These types of outfits also tend to be difficult or expensive to unlock.

Some outfits have different variations to choose from. For example, there are seven different versions of the Lynx outfit. Each one is cat-themed, but they are all different. One version simply features a hat with cat ears. Others look like futuristic, cat-like superhero costumes.

In addition to your outfit, you can choose a piece of Back Bling to equip on your character. Like outfits,

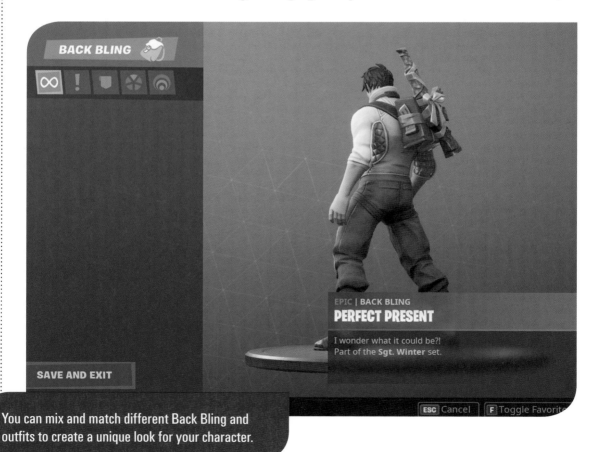

You can mix and match different Back Bling and outfits to create a unique look for your character.

Like weapons and other items you can pick up while playing *Fortnite*, skins and emotes all have different levels of rarity. Each level of rarity has a different color:

COLOR	RARITY
Gray	Common
Green	Uncommon
Blue	Rare
Purple	Epic
Orange/Gold	Legendary

With weapons and items, rarity generally indicates how powerful something is. For example, Uncommon weapons do more damage than Common ones. With customization items, rarity simply tells you how likely it is that you will run into another player with the same skin or emote. This means, for instance, that Epic and Legendary skins are much harder to get than Common or Uncommon ones.

Back Bling items can drastically change the look of your *Fortnite* fighter. Also like outfits, they range from very simple, realistic items to the goofiest things you could think of. The most basic versions of Back Bling are backpacks that come in different shapes and colors. But you can also unlock everything from a giant container of french fries to an enormous cuckoo clock.

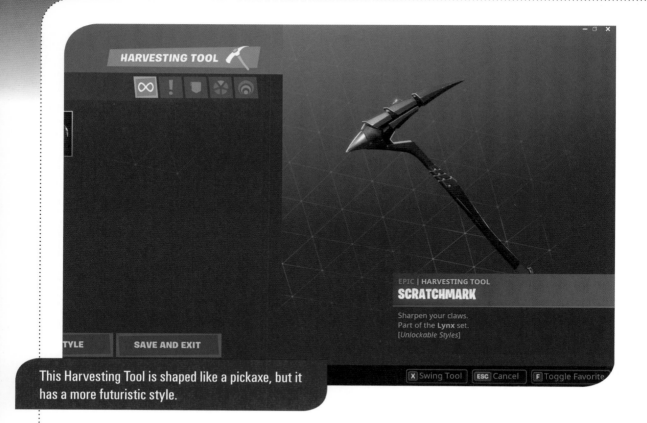

HARVESTING TOOL

EPIC | HARVESTING TOOL
SCRATCHMARK

Sharpen your claws.
Part of the **Lynx** set.
[*Unlockable Styles*]

...TYLE   SAVE AND EXIT

X Swing Tool   ESC Cancel   F Toggle Favorite

This Harvesting Tool is shaped like a pickaxe, but it has a more futuristic style.

Would you like to strap an enormous piece of sushi to your character's back? Or a disco ball? Back Bling will allow you to do all of that and much more.

You can also find a huge variety of different skins to change the look of your Harvesting Tool. The most basic version of the Harvesting Tool is the standard pickaxe. Every player starts with this. But the more you play, the more tools you will unlock to help you knock down houses, trees, and other objects to collect building materials.

Some Harvesting Tools look like tools you might use in real life. They include hammers, axes, crowbars, and other versions of the pickaxe. However, most Harvesting Tool skins are a lot crazier than that. You can equip a giant lollipop or carry a whole basketball hoop. You can knock down trees with a balloon animal or a paint roller. You can bust cars apart with a guitar or a huge magnifying glass.

You will use a glider at the start of each *Fortnite* match. This allows you to safely glide to your starting location after jumping out of the Battle Bus. It should come as no surprise that you can customize the look of your glider just like you can almost every other item in *Fortnite*. Most glider skins have the same basic shape. The main things that vary between them are their colors and patterns. For example, you might get a soccer-themed glider skin. It is decorated with a soccer ball pattern on top and a soccer field pattern on its wings. A pirate-themed glider features a skull and crossbones.

Of course, it wouldn't be *Fortnite* without some really wacky options. Some skins completely change the shape of your glider. The Glidurrr skin is shaped like a giant hamburger with a cartoon face. Flappy Flyer makes your glider look like a massive chicken. Other skins can turn your glider into a paper airplane, a helicopter, and more. You can even glide down from the Battle Bus using a shark with a laser strapped to its back!

Glider skins aren't the only way to give your character some style when jumping from the Battle Bus. You can also unlock skins for something called contrails. Contrails are the visual effects that surround your character when you are skydiving. The default style for your contrails is white lines that trail behind you as you fall. But skins will let you change these lines into flames, bubbles, hearts, and much more.

If you want to decorate your weapons and vehicles in *Fortnite*, you will need to unlock some wraps. A wrap looks like a roll of cloth or wrapping paper. Each one displays a different pattern. Some have multicolored, textured appearances. Others are solid colors. You can select a different wrap for each of the following categories: Vehicles, Assault Rifles, Shotguns, SMGs, Sniper Rifles, and Pistols. When

EDIT STYLE

SAVE AND EXIT

RARE | WRAP
ARCTIC CAMO

Show your style.

A wrap is a great way to add some color to your weapons.

you pick up any items that fall into these categories, they will be decorated with your chosen wrap. So, for example, if you equip a bright-red wrap in the Pistol slot, all pistols you pick up in a match will be bright red. Unlike other skins, wraps cannot change the shape of the items they are being used to modify.

Fortnite's emotes are some of its most famous and well-liked customization options. You can perform these fun animations at any point during a match. They range from elaborate dance moves to simple gestures such as pumping your fist in the air or clapping your hands. These emotes are a great way to communicate with your teammates in Duos or Squads modes. They can express just about any feeling you can think of. Of course, some of them don't really communicate anything at all. They are just there to make you laugh!

Sprays are another way to communicate with other players in *Fortnite*. A spray is a piece of graffiti art

Choosing between different emotes and sprays in a match is fast and easy.

that you can place onto walls during a match. You can activate your equipped sprays using the same button you use to perform emotes. However, you'll need to be standing close to a wall for it to work.

Some sprays are symbols such as arrows and circles. Others display artwork of *Fortnite*'s characters. You can use them to decorate the structures you build. Of course, you can also spray them on enemy structures to **taunt** your rivals.

Not all of *Fortnite*'s customization options are for your character and the gear you use in-game. You can also unlock items that let you change the music that plays in menu screens and the artwork that is displayed on your screen when the game is loading. These will keep you from getting bored with hearing and seeing the same things over and over again as you play.

Chapter 3

Shopping Spree

By now, you probably have a few ideas about how you'd like to customize your own *Fortnite* character. So how do you start unlocking all of this cool gear? If you started out with the free version of *Fortnite*, you might not have any customization items available to use even after playing for hours. If you got

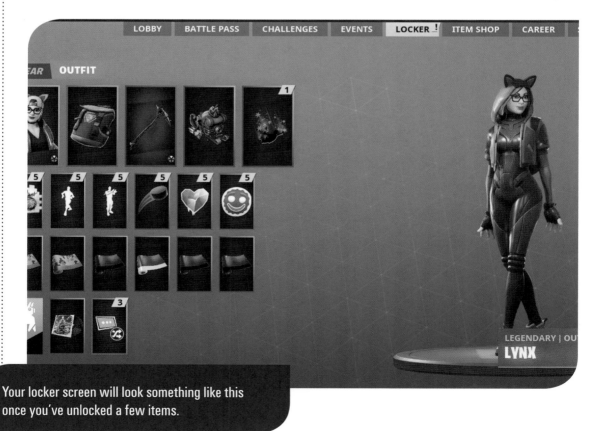

Your locker screen will look something like this once you've unlocked a few items.

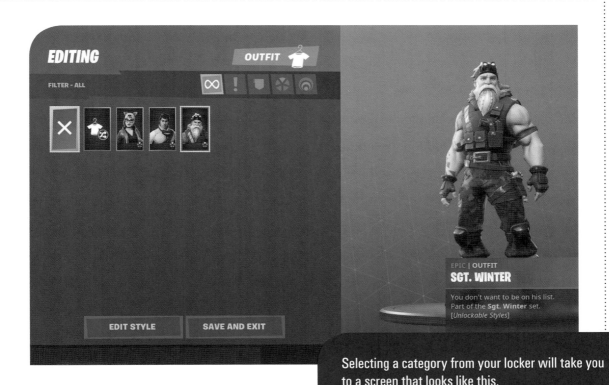

Selecting a category from your locker will take you to a screen that looks like this.

a paid version of the game, you might have started out with a few skins or emotes.

To check which items are available to you, you'll need to visit your locker. You can do this by selecting the "locker" option from the main Battle Royale menu. This screen will show you all of the different skin and emote categories. Click each one to see a list of available options for that category. If you don't have any skins or emotes to equip, the category will show a simple blue graphic. This indicates that you will have to use the default appearance. If you have items to equip, they will show up on a list for you to select from. You can also set a skin category to "random." If you do this, the game will pick a different skin from your available choices each match.

Note that you cannot set your emotes to random. You have six emote slots that you can fill with the ones you want to use most often. However, you are not limited to these six when you are in a match. When you

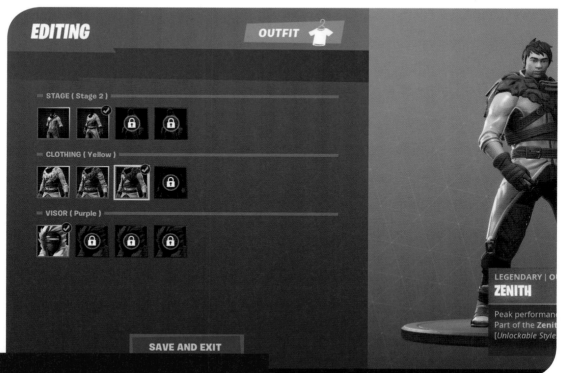

For certain outfits, you can choose "edit style" to choose between colors and other options.

Watch Your Spending

Even though it is free to download and start playing, *Fortnite* can be a very expensive game. Each individual item in the *Fortnite* item shop usually costs just a few dollars. This might not seem like a lot of money. However, if you buy a lot of items, you might be surprised to find out how much money you spend over time. A couple of dollars here and there can add up quickly!

Be sure to ask a parent or other trusted adult before purchasing V-Bucks. Try to keep track of how much you are spending. Don't waste your V-Bucks on items you only want a little bit. Instead, save them for the real must-have skins and emotes.

press the emote button in-game, you will get a chance to pick which one you want to use.

Now you know which customization options you have available to you. But they probably aren't the exact ones you are looking for. You have a few different options if you want to start collecting new skins and emotes. The simplest and fastest way is to visit the in-game item shop. You can do this from the main Battle Royale menu.

On the item shop screen, you will see a handful of different customization items for sale. The items that are available change all the time. Some of them cycle out once per day. Others are available for a few hours at a time. This means that you can always check back a little later if you don't see anything you want.

If you want to purchase something from the *Fortnite* item shop, you'll need V-Bucks. V-Bucks are *Fortnite*'s official **currency**. You can purchase them directly through the game. They cost real money, so you'll need to ask a parent or other trusted adult to use a credit card. You can buy V-Bucks in several different amounts. Some packs of V-Bucks also come with skins you can equip.

If you have enough V-Bucks in your account, it is very easy to purchase the things you want from the item shop. Simply highlight the item you are interested in and press a button. The game will ask you if you're sure. If you say yes, the item will be added to your locker.

The item shop isn't the only way to unlock new customization items in *Fortnite*. You can also earn new stuff by playing the game and completing challenges. Every couple of months begins a new "season" of *Fortnite*. Over the course of each season, players have an opportunity to move through the **tiers** of a new Battle Pass. Each tier unlocks a new set of

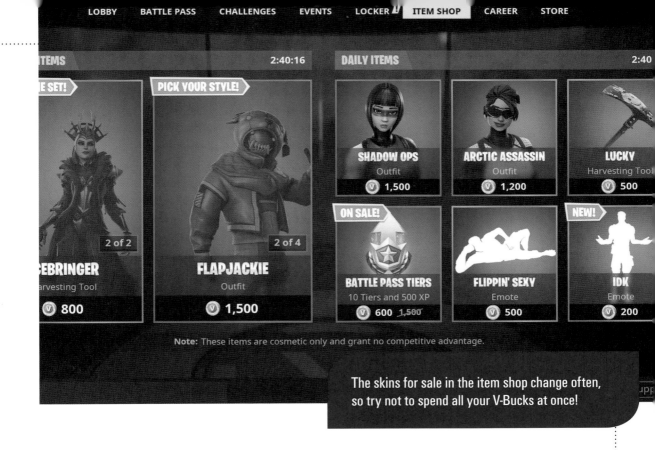

ITEMS 2:40:16

DAILY ITEMS 2:40

E SET!

PICK YOUR STYLE!

SHADOW OPS
Outfit
1,500

ARCTIC ASSASSIN
Outfit
1,200

LUCKY
Harvesting Tool
500

2 of 2

2 of 4

EBRINGER
arvesting Tool
800

FLAPJACKIE
Outfit
1,500

ON SALE!

BATTLE PASS TIERS
10 Tiers and 500 XP
600 1,500

FLIPPIN' SEXY
Emote
500

NEW!

IDK
Emote
200

Note: These items are cosmetic only and grant no competitive advantage.

The skins for sale in the item shop change often, so try not to spend all your V-Bucks at once!

customization items. There are 100 tiers in a Battle Pass. It takes a long time to reach tier 100, even if you are very good at the game.

Some items in the Battle Pass are free for all players who reach different tiers. But most of the items are only unlocked for players who have purchased a paid version of the Battle Pass. This costs 950 V-Bucks per season, or about $10 in real money. If you play *Fortnite* a lot, this is the least expensive way to unlock a lot of customization options. Reaching certain tiers will even earn you V-Bucks, so you can get some of your money back if you make it far enough by the end of the season. You can choose the "Battle Pass" option on the main Battle Royale menu screen at any time to see what tier you are at and find out which items you will unlock at each tier.

So how exactly do you move your way up the tiers? The fastest way is to complete challenges. These are specific goals you can accomplish in the game. For example, you might be challenged to eliminate four

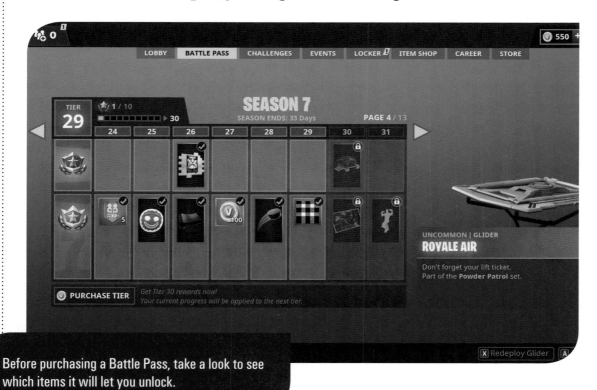

Before purchasing a Battle Pass, take a look to see which items it will let you unlock.

players using a shotgun. Or you might be challenged to simply eliminate 10 opponents using any weapon.

Some challenges are daily. You can see them listed on the left side of the main lobby screen. Here, you'll also see which Battle Pass tier you've reached and what your character level is for the season. Your level will go up as you play the game. The better you do in a match, the faster you will level up. Leveling up will help you move up the Battle Pass tiers too.

There are also weekly challenges and challenges that last through the length of a season. You can see them by choosing "Challenges" from the main Battle Royale menu. If you want to move up the tiers of a Battle Pass as quickly as you can, always keep an eye on which challenges are available. You'll want to keep these goals in mind as you play the game.

Chapter 4

The Latest and Greatest

A lot of *Fortnite* players get caught up in the rush to unlock the newest, most hyped skins and emotes. New things get added to the game with each season, so no one ever runs out of things to purchase and unlock. Chasing after cool new

A cool new glider skin is fun to look at, but it does not change the way you play the game.

Completing challenges is a great way to unlock items without spending money.

customization options can be a lot of fun. It keeps *Fortnite* players interested in the game even after they've been playing for a long time. However, it is important to remember that there is more to *Fortnite* than skins and emotes.

None of the customization options you unlock in *Fortnite* will ever change anything about the way the game plays. Wrapped weapons are not more powerful than regular ones. Players with cool outfits and gliders do not gain any special abilities. A player who doesn't spend any money on the game or unlock any customization options can be just as skilled as someone who has all of the most stylish new outfits.

Try to avoid getting jealous of friends or even random players online when they have a rare outfit or dance that you'd like to have. This kind of attitude can lead you to spend more money than you can afford chasing after new *Fortnite* items. It can also make the game less fun. Customization options are just a cool

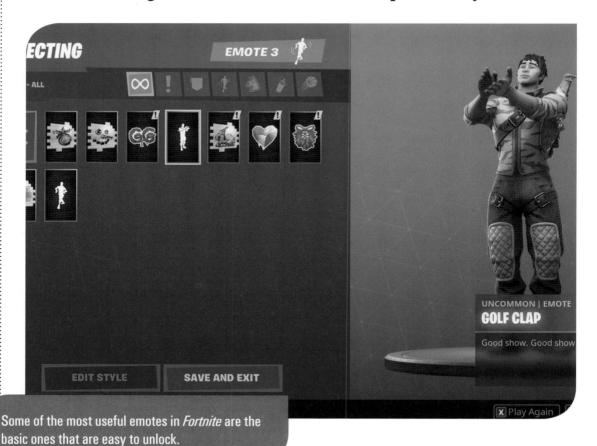

Some of the most useful emotes in *Fortnite* are the basic ones that are easy to unlock.

Showing Off Your Skills

Have you ever seen a *Fortnite* player jump out of the Battle Bus and pop open an umbrella to glide down to the ground instead of using a glider? Umbrellas are some of the coolest skins in the game. They cannot be purchased through the item shop. They can't be unlocked by moving up the tiers of a Battle Pass, either. In fact, they are completely free. You just have to be skilled enough to win one.

Umbrellas are awarded to players who achieve a Victory Royale. This is when you are the last player standing in a Battle Royale match. It takes a lot of skill to win a Victory Royale, so an umbrella is a sign that you are a truly great *Fortnite* player.

A new umbrella design gets released in each season of *Fortnite*. This means that if you want to collect them all, you will need to score a Victory Royale at least once per season.

bonus feature. The real fun of *Fortnite* comes from improving your skills, winning matches, and playing together with your friends.

Complete challenges, win matches, and move your way up the tiers of each season's Battle Pass. Even if you don't spend any money, you'll unlock some cool items and have a blast along the way!

Glossary

currency (KUR-uhn-see) a system of money

default (dih-FAWLT) the initial option selected in a game or other computer program before it is adjusted by a user

developers (dih-VEL-uh-purz) people who make video games or other computer programs

emotes (EE-mohts) animations a character can perform in an online video game to communicate with other players

taunt (TAWNT) to challenge another player by teasing them

tiers (TEERZ) ranks or levels

Find Out More

BOOKS

Cunningham, Kevin. *Video Game Designer*. Ann Arbor, MI: Cherry Lake Publishing, 2016.

Powell, Marie. *Asking Questions About Video Games*. Ann Arbor, MI: Cherry Lake Publishing, 2016.

WEBSITES

Epic Games—Fortnite
www.epicgames.com/fortnite/en-US/home
Check out the official *Fortnite* website.

Fortnite Wiki
https://fortnite.gamepedia.com/Fortnite_Wiki
This fan-made website offers up-to-date information on the latest additions to *Fortnite*.

Index

About the Author

Josh Gregory is the author of more than 125 books for kids. He has written about everything from animals to technology to history. A graduate of the University of Missouri–Columbia, he currently lives in Chicago, Illinois.